Make Mine Cold Brew:
Ideas and Recipes to Elevate your Coffee

Renae Clark

Make Mine Cold Brew: Ideas and Recipes to Elevate Your Coffee
by Renae Clark

Dilettante Living Press

Cover Design: chalk design by Albi; coffee image used under license from Storyblocks.com; cover design by Renae Clark

Table of Contents

Introduction

What is Cold Brew Coffee

Cold brew is simply coffee brewed without hot water. The temperature of the water can be anywhere from cold to room temperature. The benefits of brewing this way include less acidity, less bitterness, and a smooth bold cup of coffee. While it may seem like cold brew is the latest trend in modern coffee culture, it is in fact a renaissance of a traditional technique.

History

Various cultures have been making coffee cold for at least 400 years. Necessity is the mother of invention, and cold brew's roots appear to be entirely practical. Cold brewed coffee is thought to have originated with Dutch sailors making a coffee concentrate that was stable enough to withstand weeks at sea. Hot coffee tends to oxidize quickly, which negatively affects its flavor.

Another practical reason for brewing cold was it was sort of dangerous to make coffee over an open fire on a wooden ship. Making coffee cold may have been a way to keep from burning the ship down. Ah, leave it to the Dutch to be eminently practical

While sailing the eastern waters, Dutch style coffee seems to have found its way onto the shores of Korea and Japan. Its popularity there does not seem to have waned over the centuries, even though the Dutch themselves all but forgot their namesake brew. In Japan, the technique became known as Kyoto style coffee.

Modern Kyoto or Dutch style coffee is made with a cold drip technique, which is one of two major ways to extract coffee without heat, but more about that later.

In 19th century England, there is evidence that cold brewed coffee was common. In his lengthy exploration of the history of coffee William Ukers states "Cold infusions were common, the practise [sic] being to let them stand overnight, to be filtered in the morning, and only heated, not boiled." [1]

In 1883, a book by Poore gave these instructions:

"The most economical way of making coffee is to put the coffee into a jug and pour cold water upon it. This should be done some hours before the coffee is wanted--overnight, for instance, if the coffee be required for breakfast. The light particles of coffee will imbibe the water and fall to the bottom of the jug in course of time. When the coffee is to be used stand the jug in a saucepan of water or a bain-marie and place the outer vessel over the fire till the water contained in it boils. The coffee in this way is gently brought to the boiling point without violent ebullition, and we get the maximum extract without any loss of aroma." (Quoted in All About Coffee, Ukers p.707)[1]

Fast forward a century and we find Todd Simpson inventing the Toddy brewer in the 1960's. For years this device was synonymous with cold brew—even today former baristas can be heard referring to cold brew as a "toddy."

Some 50 years after the introduction of the Toddy, suddenly there are more products to create the perfect cold brew than you can count. One doesn't really need fancy gadgets to make a great cold brew though. Like the British of the 1800's, just let the coffee steep overnight, strain and enjoy. Yet, in a coffee crazed culture we find it hard to believe that we can't improve upon something so simple. It is a question that has prompted me to dive deep into the world of cold brew, and after a lot of experimentation and testing, this book is the result of my research.

How to Make Cold Brew

There are two main ways to make cold brew coffee, by immersion, and by drip.

Immersion

The simplest way to make a batch of cold brew coffee is by immersion. This is simply soaking coffee grounds in water for an extended period of time to extract the flavors. There are several variables that can be played around with, so let's explore some of the factors to consider when making the perfect batch.

Time

Time is one of three main variables affecting the final product. Typical brew times by immersion are 12-24 hours. Any less and you run the risk of an under extracted and weak result; any longer and you could end up with an unpleasant, over-extracted brew.

Temperature

The second main variable is temperature. Cold brew is in fact room temperature brew. While you may start with cold water (although room temperature water is also fine), extraction usually happens at room temperature, about 70-72 F for most of us.

These two variables, time and temperature form an inverse relationship. Brewing at cooler temperatures requires longer soaking times, while brewing at room temperature allows for a shorter soaking time.

Some recipes will direct you to brew in the refrigerator. In my experience this works well, especially if you extend immersion times to 16-24 hours. When brewing at room temperature, you can stick to the shorter end of the recommended range—12-18 hours. Truth be told, I have even had decent results with as little as 7 hours on the countertop, or 12 hours in the fridge. Brewing longer does create a smoother end result, but if you are pressed for time, don't get too caught up in immersion times.

Grind

The third and final major variable is the consistency of the grind. In general, finer grinds (like espresso) do not work well in cold brew as they result in a more bitter, over-extracted result. Coarse grinds work best. With less surface area than a fine grind, they can withstand the long brew times.

Just like with hot coffee, buying whole beans and grinding just before use will yield the tastiest result. While blade grinders work just fine for espresso and other finer grinds, I find it difficult to get an even coarse grind with them. I have tried pulsing, rotating, and shaking the grinder, but always end up with a few larger chunks of beans left over along with some finer sand like grinds. An uneven grind means some of your coffee will be under-extracted and some will be over-extracted.

A burr grinder can be set for the type of grind you want and delivers a more consistent result. The artisan coffee movement means there are more options for burr grinders on the market than in the past, bringing the price of some models down into a ballpark most of us can afford.

Brew in the filter bag vs. filter afterwards

Once your coffee has done its requisite soak, it's time to separate the grounds from the coffee. A paper filter placed in a cone filter does a good job of removing all sediment and leaves you with a nice clear drink. When brewing hot coffee, there is sometimes a concern by those with more sensitive palates that the paper from the filter can cause off flavors. With the cool temperatures we are dealing with, I have not noticed any off flavor in coffee strained in paper.

To make the process more convenient, some prefer to soak the coffee in a filter bag. Commercial products are available with coffee grounds packaged in what looks like large tea bags. Empty tea bags are also available online should you want to create your own coffee sachets. Shortcomings of this method are a fragile, wet bag of grounds that needs to be carefully removed from the water at the end of brewing--a lesson I learned personally when testing coffee pitcher packs. Grounds. Everywhere.

Variations include coffee socks and nut milk bags. While the intention of these is to steep the coffee and bag together in the water and then remove both, they are best used as a substitute for a paper filter for straining. Soaking in a cloth bag for the whole steep almost always imparts an off flavor that reminds me of chewing on fabric (how do I know what this even tastes like?).

If using a cloth bag, it should be boiled for a few minutes in a pan of water to clean it before first use. In experiments with organic cotton bags, I found that a pre-boil removes a lot of tiny fibers and leaves what I can only describe as a starchy residue in the pan. After several uses and washings, the bag was still giving off fibers and residue. I retired the cotton bag and moved on.

Nut milk bags are usually made of nylon fibers, and do not have the same problems as natural fibers. If you would like to soak grounds in the bag, this is least likely to taint your drink with off flavors. The disadvantage is not everyone wants to soak their coffee in a synthetic polymer bag.

Whichever type of bag you use, whatever time you saved by brewing in the bag will be lost cleaning all of the grounds out of the seams of your bag. You need to wash carefully and dry thoroughly between uses. No one wants to make coffee with a moldy bag that has old coffee grounds stuck in the nooks and crannies.

A potential solution to the problems of fabric bags are pitchers with built in infuser baskets. The filter baskets are usually made of stainless steel. While there is some school of thought that coffee should not contact metal, there is no consensus. The disadvantage of these baskets is if you use finer ground coffee (like already ground from the store), some of the smaller particles may end up as sediment at the bottom of your cup. If you coarse grind your coffee from whole beans, sediment can usually be avoided.

An even better solution is to use a French press coffee maker. Place your coarse grounds in the pitcher and add water. Place the lid on with the plunger all the way up and let it steep for 12-24 hours. After brewing, gently push the plunger down until you meet resistance. Let the coffee settle a minute or two after plunging to let any sediment settle, and then pour yourself a cup of coffee. This gives similar results to infuser pitchers, but your coffee isn't touching metal the whole time it's brewing.

Ratio

Coffee enthusiasts debate the perfect ratio of coffee grounds to water. This method certainly takes more coffee than hot brewed. The best ratio is 1 part coffee to 3 parts water. To put this in kitchen friendly terms, about 1 cup of coffee to 3 cups of water. This ratio yields a concentrate that can be diluted 50/50 with water when serving.

Of course, you can adjust that ratio up or down to suit your taste. I have found that 2 generous coffee scoops of grounds in about 8 oz. of water yields something near ready to drink. Adding a few ice cubes to the room temperature solution dilutes it to near perfect.

Even though you may gasp at the amount of coffee needed to create a batch of cold brew, it is always best to err on the side of too strong. A weak brew as a result of being stingy with the coffee is a wasted brew. You can always dilute a brew that is too strong, but you can't fix one that is too weak.

Cold Drip

Cold drip is another method for extracting coffee without heat. This method is also known as Dutch or Kyoto coffee. Traditional brewers are elaborate glass and wooden towers. Modern products have simplified things greatly and are much less fragile and less expensive.

No matter what the apparatus, the idea is to very slowly drip water through the grounds. By slowly, we are talking about a drop every second or two. Despite how slowly the water drips through, the great advantage of this method is that your coffee is ready in a fraction of the time it takes to extract by immersion. Brew times for cold drip can be as little as 3-4 hours. Cold drip coffee uses about the same amount of coffee grounds as immersion, however with a medium grind instead of coarse.

While it seems counter-intuitive that cold water dripping through coffee grounds should yield a similar result as soaking coffee for 12-24 hours, it does work. The coffee grounds become saturated with water, and as each drop of water is added to the saturated grounds from above, a droplet of coffee is released from the grounds to the vessel below. Each drop that falls from the coffee grounds has likely been soaking for several minutes before being displaced by a fresh drop.

Drip over ice

The flavors that distinguish cold brew from iced coffee are in large part due to the lack of certain flavor compounds that are only extracted by hot water. Some people believe you can have your cake and eat it too--extract these compounds and cool them quickly so they don't evaporate. This is not truly cold brew. You may see this technique called Japanese pour over ice, or just plain drip over ice.[2]

With this method, a cone filter is set over a cup of ice. A filter with coffee is placed in the cone, and hot water (taken to the boil and then left to cool for a minute or two) is slowly poured into the cone in a circular motion around the edges.

We all know what happens when you put near boiling water over ice, so why would we risk diluting our coffee like this? Like everything cold brew, patience is a virtue. By pouring the hot water in slowly, it drips through the cone slowly. When the coffee contacts the ice cubes drip by drip, the ice does not melt as rapidly as it would if you poured the hot water in quickly. Of course, some dilution is inevitable, and to make this work, you should add enough coffee to the filter to make a very strong brew. If you normally use one scoop, use two.

Serving it Hot

Historically, cold brew was served warmed, but as we learned in the introduction, even 150 years ago they knew better than to bring it to a boil. Coffee was gently heated, or heated in a bain-marie (a water bath, which provides gentle heating). My first introduction to cold brew in the 1990's included the instruction to brew it cold, but dilute it with hot water.

In coffee houses these days, cold brew is almost always served cold, usually iced. It can be heated, although diluting with hot water may not be the best option. Rather, the historical method of gently warming the coffee is better. Don't microwave it. You can gently warm it in a sauce pan, in a heat proof container (like a mason jar) nestled in a water bath, or in a double boiler. Do not bring it to a boil, but rather, just hot enough to drink.

The coffee shop near my house now offers steamed cold brew. This is another idea for warming your cold brew. Prepare your cold brew, then use the steam wand of your espresso maker to heat the brew.

Cold Brew FAQ

Cold Brew vs. Iced Coffee—What's the difference?

Cold brew coffee is made with coffee grounds and water without using heat. Once brewed, it can be drunk cold, or gently heated. In contrast, iced coffee is coffee brewed with hot water that has been cooled.

It is important to distinguish cold brew from iced coffee because the flavors are different. There are hundreds of flavor components in coffee, some of which are only extracted with heat. These compounds are often volatile, meaning they evaporate quickly, which gives you the fragrant aroma of hot coffee. These are also thought to be the components that cause coffee to taste bitter. By brewing cold, we avoid the bitter compounds, resulting in the smooth coffee that cold brewing is known for.

A cup of coffee consists of coffee solubles dissolved in water. The solubles include oils, acids and aromatic molecules[4] and are extracted from coffee beans during brewing. At hotter temperatures, more solubles dissolve. Heat also causes the aromatic molecules to evaporate--contributing to the aroma. At hotter temperatures, the oils can also oxidize causing sourness, and the acids to degrade causing bitterness.[4]

When we brew at room temperature or cooler, there are fewer solubles extracted. To compensate, we use more grounds and brew for longer. Due to lower temperatures, oxidation and degradation happen much more slowly and as a result, we don't have the same bitterness or sourness.

While on the subject of extraction, later on in the recipe section we will be using dairy and alcohol to extract coffee solubles. Dairy is composed of fats and water. This will extract both water soluble and fat soluble components of coffee.[5] Alcohol extracts water and alcohol soluble compounds from coffee. As I am sure you are beginning to see, for something as simple as coffee there are lots of variables and nuances.

Are there benefits to drinking coffee?

Coffee used to be maligned, but it turns out that it has plenty of health benefits. It contains vitamins, (especially B vitamins), minerals, and antioxidants like polyphenols, hydrocinnamic acid, and chlorogenic acids. Coffee is also associated with lower incidences of diseases such as diabetes, Alzheimers, Parkinsons, and some cancers.

Chlorogenic Acids

Chlorogenic acids have been in the press in recent years as a weight loss aid. They are associated with stimulating bile, reducing gallstones, and increasing metabolism. Green coffee beans have a high concentration of chlorogenic acids, however roasting alters them. Darker roasts lose the most chlorogenic acids. Light roasts lose about 40% of these acids and medium roasts about 60%.[6] We can infer then that if you are drinking coffee for these benefits, the light to medium roasts that are often preferable in cold brew are your best bet.

Caffeine

Coffee also contains caffeine, a stimulant that helps with alertness and may help with fat loss.[7] The claim that caffeine could release fat from cells is what made me give coffee another chance after years of not drinking it.

Whether cold brew coffee has more caffeine than hot brew is debatable. Caffeine is water soluble so it does get extracted no matter the temperature. Some argue that the longer extraction times and increased proportion of coffee grounds to water yield a more caffeinated result in cold brew. It must be remembered though that the long extraction times compensate for the lower temperatures, and the high coffee to water ratios yield a concentrate that is usually diluted with water.

When it comes right down to it, when brewing at home, whether hot or cold, we can never be certain exactly how much caffeine is being extracted. Even commercial cold brews vary in caffeine content. The best advice is read the labels of commercial products. As for home brewing, assume cold brew has about as much caffeine as similar strength hot brew.

Acidity

Cold brewed coffee has about 60% less acid than hot brewed coffee. This contributes to the sweeter, smoother taste of cold brew. It is important to distinguish between pH of coffee (a lower pH equates with more acidic) and acidity as a flavor term. In the latter, we are referring to the brightness of the flavors. Since cold brewing extracts fewer acids from the coffee, the pH of cold brew is significantly less. This can be a great advantage if your stomach is sensitive to acidic foods.

What is Nitro Cold Brew?

Nitro cold brew is something that is primarily found in coffee shops on tap, or in cans in your grocery store. Borrowing from beers like stout, the coffee is infused with nitrogen gas as it comes out of the tap. Since nitrogen doesn't readily dissolve in water, it creates tiny bubbles. The infusion of nitrogen results in a drink that has a smoother, creamier mouth feel. It also slightly enhances the sweetness of the coffee.[3]

If you buy nitro cold brew in cans, you can enjoy that same creamy experience at home. One trick is to pour the coffee quickly out of the can (i.e. let it chug into your glass, don't gently pour it down the side). This will create a better foam.

If you want to make authentic nitro cold brew at home, be prepared to make an investment. Home kits for infusing coffee with nitrogen will set you back a couple hundred dollars. On the bright side, you can use the same kit for beer.

How long can cold brew be stored for?

Coffee that is never heated does not oxidize or degrade as quickly as heated coffee, which can taste off or rancid rather quickly. Because of this, many claim that cold brew can be kept in the refrigerator for up to 2 weeks. From a food safety standpoint, you will want to ensure that all of your brewing equipment is very clean (use the dishwasher) to avoid introducing microorganisms into your coffee if you would like to store for this long. Refrigeration slows the growth of microbial colonies, but they still grow. My personal rule is to not keep coffee in the refrigerator for more than one week—but it never lasts that long.

What sort of grind should I use?

Coarse grinds work well in cold brew. This will accomplish two things. If you do not have a fine filter (or perhaps you are brewing in a French press) this will reduce leftover coffee silt in your cup. Secondly, larger particles will prevent over-extraction that can occur during longer brew times. Over-extraction can lead to a more bitter tasting coffee, one of the flavors we are trying to avoid with cold brew.

What it the best roast?

Coffee comes in a variety of roasts with fancy names to go with them. We will keep it simple and say coffee can be roasted anywhere from light to dark and anything in between. What roast you use is a matter of preference. I have the best success with light to medium roasts. I find dark roasts produce a smoky cup of coffee. Some commercial coffee companies have opted to use a blend of roasts in their quest for a perfect tasting brew. Experiment with your favorite coffees to find which you prefer.

What about the origin of beans?

What types of beans to use is also a matter of personal preference. The flavor descriptors often given by tasters of cold brew include chocolate, fruit, citrus, and caramel. Any coffee beans with these flavor profiles would work well. The main regions to look to are Central and South America, and Ethiopia. Don't feel limited by this though, the best beans are the ones that taste good to you, not some coffee snob.

Some coffee websites have tools that allow you to select beans based on your preferences (roast, smoothness, flavors notes, etc.). A simple one is at equalexchange.coop and a more complex picker is at coffeebeancorral.com. Note that the latter tool is designed for selecting their green beans, but can still be useful in narrowing down single origin beans to try.

What temperature should I brew at?

We have already established that brewing cool extracts different flavors than brewing hot. Most cold brew instructions are not actually to brew cold, but at room temperature. You can brew in the refrigerator as well although I suggest a longer brew time if you do. For room temperature brew, I tend to do 12-18 hours, while when using the refrigerator, I brew for 18-24 hours. As discussed in chapter 2, we always compensate for cooler temperatures by extending time.

Coffee Ice Cubes

One great trick for the little leftovers of concentrate (if you have any) is to freeze them into ice cubes. You can use them to cool your coffee without diluting it. Another nifty trick is to place an equal volume of frozen coffee concentrate (each ice cube in a standard tray is roughly 1 Tbsp.) and room temperature water in a glass and let the cubes dissolve. Voila, coffee that is ready to drink.

Recipes

Cold brew coffee has a flavor profile that many find more pleasant than hot brewed coffee. So, it makes sense that cold brew would be a worthy substitute for coffee in recipes and beverages. As a general rule, any recipe that calls for hot brewed coffee can be substituted with cold brew.

For all the recipes that follow, cold brew concentrate refers to strong coffee brewed at a ratio of 1 part coffee to 3 parts water. Cold brew coffee refers to coffee that has already been diluted to strength—usually by adding equal parts water to the concentrate.

Flavoring your Coffee

Flavor the Beans

Coffee can be purchased in a myriad of flavors and any of these flavored coffees can be used to make cold brew. I am partial to chocolate flavored beans myself. Coffee roasters use special coffee flavoring oils on the beans shortly after roasting to achieve flavored beans. You can buy coffee flavor oils online, but it works best if you are roasting beans yourself (which in and of itself is a fun but smelly little hobby).

Two ways that are a little easier for the home user are to store your coffee with spices, or use flavored extracts.

Spices

Coffee is actually great at absorbing odors in your house. I have used it in making gardeners soap as well as in my garbage disposal to keep it fresh. We can use this absorbency to our advantage to pick up fragrances from spices.

To flavor with spices, transfer your coffee beans to a mason jar or a similar container that has a lid. Add in some whole spices and put the lid on. Allow the beans to absorb the scents of the spices for a day or two before grinding and using.

Spices and flavorings that can be purchased whole (as opposed to pre-ground) work well for this such as vanilla beans, dried orange peels, crystallized ginger, cardamom, whole cloves, nutmeg, cinnamon sticks, and anise seeds.

For vanilla flavored coffee, use a ratio of roughly 1 cup of coffee beans with 3 vanilla beans. If you split the beans open they will release more flavors. After infusing your coffee, you can remove the beans and use them for something else (homemade vanilla extract, vanilla sugar, or even vanilla liqueur).

- For cinnamon flavored coffee, you can also use a ratio of 2-3 sticks of cinnamon per cup of coffee. Two to three nutmeg cloves does the trick for a cup of beans

- If you are using cloves or anise, about 1 T. of the whole spice is a good starting point

- Eight to 10 cardamom seeds (remove the outer shells) per cup of coffee

- Dried citrus peels can be used at ¼ cup of peels to 1 c. of coffee beans

- Crystallized ginger is more pungent, and I would use about 1/8 cup of ginger to 1 c. of beans.

All of the above are conservative amounts. My preference is for flavors to take a backseat to the coffee. They should create new nuances, not be overpowering. To adjust the above flavorings to your preferences, you can use more spices to create a more flavorful bean. Or, you can continue to store your beans and spices together for a longer period of time. The beans will pick up more flavors over time. Just remember that a few weeks after roasting, coffee beans start to lose their freshness so don't store them for too long!

Extracts

The other option for flavoring beans is to apply some extracts to them. You can find these in the baking aisle of your grocery store. To do this, place a portion of coffee beans in a bowl or glass container—I do this right before grinding—and sprinkle the extract over the beans. Let it soak in for several minutes, then grind.

How much extract you use depends on how strongly the extract smells. For most flavors, ½ to 1 tsp. will be about right, but peppermint extract is more potent and it is better to start with less and adjust upwards if you want a stronger flavor.

Some examples of extracts you can try (per ½ cup of coffee beans):

For vanilla, use ½ to 1 tsp.

For mint, use ¼ to ½ tsp.

For almond, use ½ tsp.

For orange, use ½ to 1 tsp.

For hazelnut use ½ to 1 tsp.

Note: There are two types of extracts available, with or without alcohol. The non-alcoholic versions are usually glycerin based. Since these are syrupy, they don't work as well for flavoring beans. Alcoholic extracts flavor the beans by soaking into the beans, and then the alcohol evaporates off a bit.

And speaking of alcohol, there is no reason not to get a bit creative with this technique. Use a teaspoon or two of coffee, hazelnut, or almond liqueurs to flavor your beans.

Flavor the Brew

Flavoring coffee beans is one way to infuse your coffee with complementary tones. You can also add flavoring as you brew. Any of the spices used above can be ground together with your beans and used to infuse the water directly with their flavors.

If you grind your beans yourself, just throw the whole spices into a blade grinder along with the beans and give it a whirl. If you use a burr grinder, it will work better to grind your spices separately in a spice grinder. You could also use pre-ground spices, though they are usually less flavorful then freshly ground spices.

Combine coffee and spices in your immersion container and let the coffee steep your usual length of time. Strain and enjoy.

Aside from spices, you can use vanilla beans, cacao nibs, or toasted coconut to flavor your brew with this method.

When brewing hot coffee, it is possible to toast nuts such as almonds and add them to the filter basket with the coffee grounds. This does not have the same effect with cold brew.

I don't recommend soaking toasted nuts in cold brew immersion techniques. The reason for this is that soaking nuts is the first step in making a nut milk. The initial soaking plumps them up and removes some of the phytic acid from them. The soaking water is usually discarded at this point and then fresh water is added to make the milk. If we were to soak nuts in with the coffee grounds, we would be making coffee out of the water that is usually discarded. I am not a food scientist, so I can't offer a better explanation, except that intuitively it just seems wrong to me to brew with water you would otherwise toss. If you want to try adding toasted ground nuts while brewing, I would recommend using a drip brewer where the water passes through the grounds relatively quickly. Better yet would be to stick to nut extracts (e.g. almond or hazelnut) or flavored syrups.

Toasted Coconut Cold Brew Coffee

½ c. coconut flakes

½ c. coffee beans

2 c. water

Toast ½ c. of coconut in a skillet. Place coconut in the pan over medium heat and stir frequently until the coconut takes on a golden color around the edges. Watch closely, as they can quickly become over-toasted (completely golden brown). Remove from the heat and place coconut in your immersion container. Grind your coffee beans and add to the immersion container. Top with 2 cups of water and let soak for up to 24 hours. Strain out the grounds and coconut. Dilute with water to taste.

To amp up the coconut flavor, try serving coconut cold brew with coconut flavored creamer, coconut milk, or coconut cream. You can also add a little raw coconut oil and froth it.

Cacao Cold Brew Coffee

½ c. coffee beans

2 c. water

¼ c. cacao nibs

Grind coffee beans and add to your immersion container. Add cacao nibs and top with 2 cups water. Let it brew for up to 24 hours. Strain out the coffee and nibs. Dilute with water to taste.

Note: if you can't find cacao nibs, you can substitute 1 T. cacao powder.

Cinnamon Cold Brew Coffee

½ c. coffee beans

2 c. water

1 stick cinnamon

Grind the coffee beans and add to the immersion container. Add cinnamon stick and top with 2 c. water. Let steep for up to 24 hours. Strain out the grounds and cinnamon. Dilute with water to taste.

Serving suggestion: Serve Cinnamon Cold Brew over ice and top with a dollop of whip cream and a sprinkle of cinnamon

Flavored Syrups

There are a gajillion flavored syrups out there and I could spend the next 40 pages giving you recipes for each one. But flavored syrups are so simple, there is no need. Instead, here are some basic formulas with an example or two, and ideas for modifying it to your favorite flavor.

Homemade coffee syrups are just simple syrups with different flavorings. The most basic simple syrup is made from equal parts water and sugar. Adding a little bit of corn syrup is optional, but can help prevent the sugar from crystallizing. Simple syrup can be stored in the refrigerator for several weeks and is also a useful addition to your cocktail bar.

If you like your syrup a little thicker, use up to 2 parts sugar and 1 part water. For a thinner syrup, you can use 2 parts water and 1 part sugar. Simple syrup is pretty hard to mess up.

Basic Flavored Simple Syrup

½ c. sugar

½ c. water

1 tsp. flavoring extract of your choice

Combine water and sugar in a saucepan and bring to a simmer over medium heat. Adjust heat to keep at a gentle simmer (we don't want a hard boil). Simmer for 5-10 minutes until slightly thickened. Stir in the extract and remove from heat.

You can use whatever flavor extract you want including vanilla, almond, peppermint, orange, maple, hazelnut, coconut and more. If you are using a strong flavoring like peppermint, start with a ½ tsp. and adjust up from there to suit your taste buds.

Cinnamon Brown Sugar Syrup

You can alter the flavors of your syrup by playing around with different types of sugars as in this next variation.

½ c. brown sugar

½ c. water

¼ tsp. vanilla extract

¼ tsp. cinnamon

Place all ingredients in a saucepan and bring to a simmer. Let simmer for 5-10 minutes until slightly thickened.

Basic Infused Simple Syrup

You can infuse simple syrups with herbs and spices. These syrups have a shorter shelf life, just a couple weeks in the refrigerator, but you can wildly expand the flavor options beyond extracts. Try cardamom, cinnamon sticks, cloves, dried orange peel, berries, or lavender.

½ c. sugar

5 oz. water

¼ c. whole herbs or spices

The first step is to create an herbal tea. Place water and the herb or spices in a saucepan and bring to a boil. Turn off the heat and let steep for 10 minutes. Strain out the herbs/spices.

Measure out ½ c. of your herbal tea and return to the heat. Add the sugar and bring to a simmer for 5-10 minutes until the sugar is dissolved and it is slightly thickened. Keeps for 2 weeks in the refrigerator.

Caramel Simple Syrup

Note: wearing long sleeves when making caramel can help to protect skin against potential burns.

1 c. sugar

5 oz. water

½ tsp. vanilla extract

1 T. corn syrup, optional

Place the sugar and corn syrup (if using) in a tall sided pan and moisten the sugar with a couple tablespoons of the water. Reserve the rest of the water.

Cook the sugar over medium heat without stirring until the sugar starts to turn golden around the edges of the pan. Swirl gently to distribute the color and remove from heat when the color is light amber. The caramel continues to get darker in the hot pan until you add the water in the next step, so always remove from the heat just a little before you think the color is correct!

Slowly and carefully add the remaining water. It will splatter and erupt a bit so do be careful as hot sugar causes nasty burns. Stir until combined, and then stir in the vanilla. Let it cool and store in the refrigerator for up to several weeks.

Rhode Island Coffee Milk

2 T. coffee syrup (see recipe on next page)

8 oz. milk

Stir the coffee syrup into the milk and enjoy the official state drink of Rhode Island

24

Coffee Syrup

1 c. cold brew, diluted to regular strength (i.e. not a concentrate)

¾ c. sugar

¼ tsp. vanilla, optional

Place all ingredients in a saucepan over medium heat. Bring just to the boil and then reduce to a simmer. Simmer for 10-15 minutes until the syrup has thickened slightly. Remove from the heat and let cool. Store for 2-3 weeks in the refrigerator.

Spiced Syrup

½ c. water

½ c. sugar

1 T. peeled and grated fresh ginger

1 stick cinnamon

1 tsp. whole cloves

Place all ingredients in a saucepan over medium heat. Bring just to the boil and then reduce to a simmer. Gently simmer for 5 minutes and then remove from heat and let steep for another 30 minutes. Strain into a jar or bottle. Store in the refrigerator for 2-3 weeks.

Flavored Creamers

Making your own creamers is nearly as easy as making your own syrups. These last about a week in the refrigerator. An important caveat to that is always make sure that your milk product has a "best by" date that is at least a week out. If its best buy date is sooner than that, your creamer will expire on the same date as the dairy.

I use half in half in these recipes because it is half cream, half milk. This is the best of both worlds, offering some creaminess with only some of the calories. You can substitute heavy cream or milk if you want a richer or thinner creamer respectively.

Vanilla Creamer

1 c. half and half

4 T. Sugar

1 tsp. vanilla extract

1 vanilla bean, split

Warm the half and half with all ingredients until the sugar dissolves. Remove from heat and let the bean steep for another 10-15 minutes. Remove the bean. Transfer the creamer to a jar or bottle and store in the refrigerator for up to a week.

Caramel Creamer

1 c. half and half

3 T. caramel simple syrup (see recipe in previous section)

Warm the milk with the caramel syrup stirring occasionally until the syrup is thoroughly dissolved. Remove from heat and transfer to a jar or bottle. Store in the refrigerator for up to a week.

Coconut Creamer

1 c. coconut milk

3 T. simple syrup

½ tsp. vanilla extract

¼ c. toasted coconut

Place the coconut in a small pan over medium low heat and toast until the coconut is golden around the edges. Stir often to make sure the coconut doesn't burn.

Add the coconut milk and simple syrup and bring to a simmer. Turn off the heat and let steep 30 minutes. Strain out the coconut.

Add the vanilla extract and transfer the creamer to a jar. Store in the refrigerator for up to a week.

Mocha Creamer

1 c. half and half

1 T. cocoa powder

1 tsp. espresso powder

1/3 c. simple syrup

In a small saucepan, combine simple syrup, cocoa powder and espresso powder and stir to make a paste. Add half and half and heat over medium low heat until the syrup and powders are dissolved. Remove from the heat and let cool. Store in a jar or bottle. Keeps in the refrigerator for up to a week.

Peppermint Cocoa Creamer

Follow the recipe for mocha creamer, but omit the espresso powder. Add ¼ tsp. peppermint extract when you remove from the heat.

Chocolate Hazelnut Creamer

1 c. half and half

1/3 c. simple syrup

1 tsp. hazelnut extract

2 tsp. cocoa powder

Stir cocoa powder into the simple syrup until well combined and free of clumps. Stir into the half and half and gently heat, stirring occasionally, until the syrup/powder mixture is well combined. Remove from the heat and add the hazelnut extract. Store in the fridge for up to one week.

Maple Creamer

1 c. half and half

¼ c. maple syrup (real maple syrup, not pancake syrup)

½ tsp. vanilla extract

Combine all ingredients in a small saucepan, heat cream and maple syrup and stir until maple syrup is fully dissolved. Do not bring to a boil. Stir in the vanilla. Store in jar or bottle in the fridge for up to one week.

Now that you have all those yummy creamers, let's channel your inner barista.

Vanilla Sweet Cream Cold Brew

8 oz. cold brew coffee

2 T. vanilla creamer, see recipe above

Add creamer to cold brew and serve over ice.

Iced Mocha #1

8 oz. cold brew coffee

2 T. mocha creamer

1 T. milk

Combine all ingredients and serve over ice.

Other Add-Ins

Making flavored syrups and creamers is simple, but you can change up the flavor of your coffee just by adding in other sweeteners or creamy liquids. This section looks at different sweeteners, milks, and fats that can take your cold brew to the next level.

Sweeteners

There are lots of options for sweetening your drink. Sugar takes many forms, some of which bring different flavors to the table including coconut sugar and brown sugar. Any of them can be made into a simple syrup using a ratio of 1 cup sugar to 1 cup water.

Simple syrups like the ones created in chapter 5 can be made without any flavorings and used to sweeten coffee. The beauty of simple syrups is that they will keep for about a month in the fridge and you can use them in cocktails as well.

Coconut sugar has a similar taste to brown sugar. It has been touted as a healthier sugar, if such a thing is possible. This is largely due to the fact that it has a lower glycemic index than regular sugar, so it doesn't cause quite the same blood sugar spike. It also contains inulin, which is a prebiotic fiber, and some trace minerals.

Brown sugar adds a slight caramel sweetness to the party and can be a nice variation from white sugar. Brown sugar is sugar and molasses.

Honey is interesting in that the flavor can vary depending on what flowers and plants the bees have been exposed to (clover, wildflower, etc.). Store bought honey has been refined and has a more consistent flavor.

Honey can also be infused with different flavors like lavender or cinnamon. Just add about 1-2 T. of *dried* herb or spice per 1 c. of honey in a jar and let it sit for a few days before straining out the herb. Be sure to use dried herbs so you don't introduce water to the honey, which will shorten its shelf life. Some people gently warm the honey and herbs to shorten infusion time to about 30 minutes. If you choose to heat the honey and herbs, you can strain out the herbs/spices once the mixture has cooled.

Agave nectar is an alternative sweetener to regular sugar. It dissolves well in cold drinks. The flavor is not too different from sugar, but with perhaps a touch more of a caramel note. One benefit of agave is that it is sweeter than sugar, so you can use about 1/3 less of it.

Maple syrup comes from the sap of certain varieties of maple trees. It is a tasty and natural sweetener with a unique flavor.

Cocoa Honey Cold Brew

8 oz. cold brew coffee

2 T. mocha creamer

1 tsp. honey

Combine all ingredients and stir. Serve over ice.

Milks and Creamers

Adding a little milk to your coffee used to mean adding a little cow's milk. Now there are several options, which is a boon to those who are sensitive to dairy. Milk choices include almond, cashew, hemp, coconut, soy, coconut cream, and the list of non-dairy options is ever expanding.

But don't forget the humble cow, variations in dairy include cream, half and half, milk, condensed milk, and evaporated milk.

Frothing is something that is often done in coffee shops to create a layer of foamy cream. The bubbles are often achieved with the steam wand of the espresso machine. You can also purchase frothers that look like miniature immersion blenders and work surprising well. They can be used with cold or warm (not hot) milk.

For any of the recipes below, you can substitute a non-dairy milk.

Creamy Coconut Cold Brew

8 oz. cold brew, diluted to preferred strength

2 oz. coconut cream

Place coffee and coconut cream in a blender and give it a few pulses. Pour over ice. Optional, add a sprinkle of cinnamon or cocoa powder on top.

Cool Latte

4 oz. milk

4 oz. cold brew

Froth milk and add to cold brew. Add ice if desired.

Spiked Cream

Whipped cream can be flavored with liqueurs and extracts and added to coffee.

1 c. whipping cream

1 T. orange liqueur (e.g. Grand Marnier, Triple Sec, Orange Curacao)

½ tsp. vanilla extract

Whip the cream with an electric mixer (or a whisk if you are strong and patient) until soft peaks form. Add the liqueur and vanilla and whip another 10-15 seconds.

You can substitute almost any liqueur for the orange liqueur including Irish cream, Irish whiskey, rum, Kahlua, Frangelico, Amaretto, raspberry liqueur (e.g. Chambord). The possibilities are virtually endless.

Mint Cream

1 c. whipping cream

½ tsp. peppermint extract

Whip the cream with an electric mixer (or a whisk if you are patient) until soft peaks form. Add the extract and whip another 10-15 seconds.

Cold Brew Cloud

8 oz. cold brew, diluted to taste

¼ c. flavored whipped cream

Prepare cold brew and add ice if desired. Top with a generous dollop of flavored whip cream.

Peppermint Cold Brew Cloud

8 oz. cold brew coffee made with chocolate flavored beans

¼ c. peppermint flavored whipped cream

Prepare cold brew using chocolate flavored beans. Serve in a glass with ice as desired, top with a dollop of whip cream.

DIY Barista and Other Virgin Drinks

Frothing Milk: If you do not have a milk frother you can also whirl your milk in a blender, use an immersion blender, shake it in a mason jar, or even plunge it up and down in a French press.

Cold Brew Macchiato

A true macchiato is espresso with a kiss of foam on top. Here is a cold brew version.

Foam from frothed milk

12 oz. Cold brew coffee

Froth milk. Heating the milk to body temperature will help produce a more stable foam.

Pour cold brew into a glass and scoop foam onto the top of the cold brew.

Iced Caramel Latte Macchiato

Many recipes for macchiato on the internet have milk, which technically makes them latte macchiato.

1 c. frothed milk

½ c. cold brew concentrate

2 tsp. vanilla simple syrup

1 T. caramel sauce

Ice

Froth milk until foamy. Add vanilla syrup and 2 tsp. caramel syrup and pulse a few more times to blend. Stir in cold brew concentrate and add ice cubes if desired. Top with a drizzle of the remaining caramel sauce.

Iced Cinnamon Latte Macchiato

1 c. frothed milk

½ c. cold brew concentrate

2 tsp. cinnamon infused simple syrup

Ice

Froth milk until foamy. Add cinnamon simple syrup and pulse a few more times to blend. Stir in cold brew concentrate. Add ice if desired.

Iced Mocha Macchiato

1 c. frothed milk

½ c. cold brew concentrate

1 tsp. vanilla syrup

1 T. chocolate sauce + extra for drizzling

Ice

Froth milk until foamy. Add vanilla syrup and chocolate sauce and pulse a few more times to blend. Pour cold brew concentrate into milk and add ice. Drizzle with chocolate syrup.

Iced Latte

A latte is 1 part espresso and 2 parts milk (usually steamed). Cold brew concentrate makes a worthy substitute for espresso.

6 oz. milk

3 oz. cold brew concentrate

Ice

Flavored syrup as desired

Froth milk until a little foamy. Stir in cold brew concentrate and add ice.

Iced Mocha #2

A mocha is a latte with the addition of chocolate syrup.

6 oz. milk

3 oz. cold brew concentrate

Ice

1 T. chocolate syrup + more for drizzling (optional)

Stir chocolate syrup into milk to make chocolate milk. Froth milk until foamy. Add cold brew and stir. Add ice. Drizzle with chocolate syrup if desired.

Mocha Frappe

1 c. cold brew concentrate

½ c. heavy cream

½ c. milk

2 T. chocolate syrup

Optional whipped cream for topping

Mix ½ c. of the coffee concentrate with the milk. Freeze the mixture into small ice cube trays.

Blend 2 T. chocolate syrup into the heavy cream.

Place remaining ½ c. coffee concentrate, chocolate cream, and frozen milk cubes into a blender and blend until smooth.

Iced Cappuccino

A cappuccino differs a little from a latte. Lattes are 1 part espresso to 2 parts milk, while a cappuccino is 1/3 espresso, 1/3 milk, and 1/3 foam.

½ c. cold brew concentrate

1 c. milk

Ice

Froth milk until very foamy. Warming the milk to body temperature will create the best foam. Place cold brew concentrate in a glass and stir in milk. Add ice cubes.

Cold Brew Affogato

Affogato Means "drowned" in Italian and is a scoop of gelato or ice cream in espresso. In Germany, a similar treat called Eiskaffe is vanilla ice cream with espresso or strong coffee, topped with whipped cream.

For 1 serving:

1 scoop vanilla gelato (can substitute with vanilla ice cream)

½ c. cold brew coffee

1 T. liqueur (optional) Irish Cream, Grand Marnier, Frangelico, Disarrono, Kahlua

Place a scoop of gelato in a bowl and pour coffee and liqueur (if using) over top.

Variations: Use chocolate gelato for a mocha affogato.

Coconut Affogato

1 scoop coconut gelato

½ c. cold brew coffee

Toasted coconut flakes for garnish

To toast coconut, place flakes in a non-stick skillet and cook over medium heat, stirring frequently, until lightly golden around the edges.

Place scoop of coconut gelato in a cup or bowl. Pour coffee over top. Garnish with toasted coconut flakes.

Vietnamese Iced Milk Coffee

½ c. coarsely ground coffee beans

1 T. ground chicory

1 ½ c. water

¼ c. condensed milk

Ice

Place coffee, chicory and water in a clean jar. Let steep for 12-18 hours on the countertop, or 16-24 hours in the fridge. Strain the coffee and chicory through a coffee filter or coffee bag.

Place the coffee in a glass and pour condensed milk into the coffee and stir. Add ice.

Café Bombon

Café Bombon is a Spanish take on Vietnamese coffee, minus the chicory.

1 c. cold brew coffee

1/3 c. condensed milk

Place coffee in a glass and pour condensed milk over the top, letting it settle on the bottom, creating a band of milk and a band of coffee. Serve. It is custom to stir before drinking.

Iced Yeunyeung Coffee

This is a popular drink in Hong Kong and blends coffee with Hong Kong style milk tea. Authentic milk tea takes a little more effort than this short cut variation:

Step 1: Make milk tea

2 Ceylon tea bags or equivalent loose leaf tea

6 oz. Hot water

2 oz. evaporated milk

2 tsp. sugar

Bring the tea and water to a boil, and continue to boil for 5 minutes. Remove from heat and let steep another 10 minutes. Strain out the tea and stir in milk and sugar. Chill. Make a few ice cubes out of the milk tea and keep the rest chilled.

Step 2: Make the Yeunyeung coffee

3 oz. cold brew coffee

7 oz. milk tea

Frozen milk tea cubes

Combine all ingredients in a glass and serve.

Iced Melya

A melya is espresso with cocoa and honey. It may or may not contain cream. In this iced version, the warm cream helps to dissolve the honey and cocoa powder.

4 oz. cold brew concentrate

1 tsp. cocoa powder

1 tsp. honey

1 oz. heavy cream

Heat the heavy cream in a small bowl or microwave safe cup at 50% power in the microwave for 20 seconds. If the cream starts to bubble up, stop the microwave. Stir the cocoa powder into the honey and keep stirring until it becomes a paste. Stir into the warm cream and let cool for 10 minutes.

Place cold brew in a glass and stir in cream. Add ice and serve

Freddo "espresso"

This is a popular drink in Greek coffee houses. It is made with foamed espresso. A little sugar can be added if you prefer a sweeter drink. Cold brew concentrate substitutes for the espresso in this recipe.

4 oz. cold brew concentrate

Ice

Sugar (optional to taste)

Add room temperature cold brew concentrate to a cocktail shaker. Add 1-2 ice cubes. Shake vigorously for a minute or until nice and frothy. Strain coffee into a glass with ice.

Variation: To make a freddo cappuccino, add 8 oz. of frothed milk to the cold brew concentrate. The milk should be frothed at body temperature (heat briefly in the microwave until it feels like baby formula temperature) and allowed to cool a few minutes so it doesn't melt all the ice.

Mazagran—Iced Coffee Lemonade

Mazagran originated in Algeria, but has also become popular in parts of Europe. It is especially popular in Portugal. The recipe varies depending on who you ask, with some adding a hint of lemonade to espresso, and at the other extreme a shot of espresso is added to lemonade. This one walks the middle ground and makes an interesting alternative to iced tea. This recipe makes two servings.

Step 1: Make lemonade

½ c. freshly squeezed lemon juice

¼ c. simple syrup

¾ c. water

Stir the lemon juice together with the simple syrup. Add the water and stir. Adjust with additional simple syrup as needed (depends how tart your lemons are).

Step 2: Make the Mazagran

2/3 c. lemonade

1/3 c. cold brew coffee

Stir lemonade and coffee in a tall glass and fill with ice. You may optionally add a splash of rum.

Tipsy Cold Brew: Liqueurs and Cocktails

In this book, we steep coffee beans in water, in dairy, and here in alcohol. Herbalists use alcohol to extract herbs in a process called tincturing. You can use the same core methods to tincture coffee beans. This isn't so exciting, but mix it with a little simple syrup and let it age a bit, and suddenly you have homemade coffee liqueur.

Coffee Liqueur

2 c. high proof vodka (100 proof)

½ c. whole coffee beans

A few drops lemon extract (optional)

½ c. simple syrup or coffee syrup (see recipe in flavored syrups section)

Sanitize a mason jar by running it through a hot dishwasher cycle, or by pouring a little boiling water in the jar and dumping it out (pick up the jar with a towel or oven mitts if doing this—it heats up quickly).

Add the first 3 ingredients to the jar and put a lid on. Let the beans steep for 3-5 days in a cool dark place, shaking once or twice a day.

Strain the beans and return the alcohol to the jar. Stir in the simple syrup. For an added coffee kick, add coffee syrup from the recipe in this book instead.

Place the lid back on and let the mixture age for at least 6 more weeks. Homemade liqueurs get mellower the longer you let them age, so don't be too eager to take a nip!

Variation: Add ¼ c. cacao nibs to the coffee when tincturing (steeping in vodka) for a chocolate coffee liqueur.

Cocktails

Coffee is used as a mixer in a variety of cocktails. Cold brew makes a great mixer as it keeps in the fridge for a week without changing much in flavor. This means it is always on hand when you need to mix, shake or stir a little something up.

Some liquors that pair well with coffee include Irish cream, Irish whiskey, hazelnut liqueur (Frangelico), almond liqueur (Amaretto, Disarrono), Orange curacao, Rum, Crème de Menthe, Chocolate mint liqueur, and of course Kahlua.

Almond Delight

½ oz. brandy

¼ oz. amaretto

1 oz. cold brew coffee

Put all in a shaker with ice. Shake and strain into a glass. Top with a dollop of whip cream.

CocoCream Coffee

1 oz. cold brew coffee concentrate

1 oz. cream

½ oz. coconut rum

Combine all ingredients and stir.

Irish Co-co-fee

6 oz. coffee

1 oz. milk

2 tsp. chocolate syrup

½ oz. Irish whiskey

Combine all ingredients and stir.

Cold Brew Martini

1.5 oz cold brew concentrate

1.5 oz vodka

1 oz coffee liqueur

Simple syrup, optional

Ice

Combine the first three ingredients in a martini shaker with ice cubes. Shake for several seconds—this will make the drink have a nice foam on top. Strain into a martini glass.

You can optionally add a little simple syrup to sweeten it up. Kick it up a notch with flavored simple syrups like orange or mint.

Hazelnut Cafe

6 oz. cold brew coffee

1 oz. coffee liqueur

½ oz. hazelnut liqueur

Ice

Combine the first three ingredients in a martini shaker with ice cubes. Shake and strain into a glass. You can optionally top with a little whipped cream.

Creamy Spiked Coffee

6 oz. cold brew

1 oz. chocolate vodka

1 T. coffee creamer

Ice

Combine all ingredients in a tall glass and stir. Add ice.

Irish Dream Cream

6 oz. cold brew concentrate

½ oz. half and half

1 oz. Irish Cream

Ice

Combine the first three ingredients in a glass and stir. Add ice.

Treats with Cold Brew

In the epic Modernist Cuisine, Nathan Myhrvold and co. delve deep into coffee and determine that cold infusing milk or cream is the best way to flavor desserts using dairy. This opens up a whole world of experimentation with classic treats. No creamy treat is more beloved than ice cream.

Cold Brew Ice Cream

1.5 cups milk

1.5 cups heavy cream

3/4 cups sugar

3 eggs

½ tsp. vanilla extract

1 cup whole coffee beans

Directions:

1. Crush the coffee beans as directed above. Place in a jar and cover with the cream. Put a lid on and place in the fridge to steep for 20-24 hours. This will be thick—try to stir or swirl the mixture a few times during the steeping process so coffee and cream is thoroughly combined.

2. Strain the cream from the coffee through a fine mesh strainer. Set aside in the fridge.

3. Place milk in a saucepan over medium heat and bring just to a simmer.

4. Whisk eggs and sugar together in a separate heat proof bowl.

5. Gradually add the heated milk to the egg mixture, whisking constantly. Tip: Add your milk very slowly at first to prevent scram-

bling the eggs. Once the eggs are warmed by the milk, you can add the milk a little faster.

6 .Return the milk and egg mixture to the saucepan and cook over medium heat, stirring constantly, until slightly thickened. This takes 10-15 minutes. You can add 1/2 teaspoon vanilla extract at this point if desired.

7. Let the milk mixture cool for 5-10 minutes, then stir in the coffee infused cream.

8. Let the ice cream mixture chill in the fridge until cold.

9. Process the mixture in your ice cream maker, following your manufacturer's directions.

Makes 1 quart

Cold Brew Cardamom Ice Cream Variation

Cardamom is sometimes added to coffee in the Middle East. This ice cream is inspired by those flavors.

Follow the previous recipe for cold brew ice cream. In step 3, place 8-10 cardamom seeds (remove them from the pods) in the milk. Bring to the simmer and then remove from the heat and let steep 10 minutes. Continue with step 4. In step 5, strain the cardamom seeds out of the milk and add to the egg mixture as directed. Continue with the rest of the recipe.

Mocha Ice Cream Variation

Coffee and chocolate are a classic ice cream flavor, and admittedly was my gateway to coffee.

Follow the cold brew ice cream recipe. In step 3, start with ¼ c. of cocoa powder in the pan and add a splash of milk. Stir to make a paste. Add another splash of milk and stir, then add the rest of the milk. Heat the milk as directed and continue with the rest of the recipe.

Irish Mocha Milkshake

This grown up milkshake is inspired by the Irish Cream milkshakes I used to have at Sophie's Cosmic Café in Vancouver.

4 scoops (about 1 ½ cups) vanilla ice cream (you can also use chocolate ice cream and omit the chocolate syrup)

1 oz. Irish cream liqueur

3 oz. cold brew coffee

1 T. chocolate syrup

Combine all ingredients in a blender and blend until smooth.

Mocha Syrup

This variation of chocolate syrup is delicious over ice cream

1 c. cold brew coffee

1 c. sugar

2/3 c. cocoa powder

1 tsp. vanilla extract

Combine the coffee, sugar, and cocoa powder in a small saucepan and place over medium heat. Heat, stirring frequently with a whisk, until it come to a simmer. Remove from heat, stir in vanilla, and store in the fridge for up to 2 weeks.

White Chocolate Coconut Truffles

4 oz white chocolate, coarsely chopped

¼ c. heavy cream

1 ½ tsp. coconut oil*

½ c. coconut, toasted

1 T. chopped coffee beans

Place chopped coffee beans in a jar. Add cream and swirl to combine. Let steep in the fridge for 20-24 hours, swirling occasionally (it will be thick). Strain and set aside.

Place chopped white chocolate in a heatproof bowl. Heat the cream and coconut oil in a small saucepan until just to the simmer. Pour the cream mixture over the white chocolate and let sit for 1-2 minutes. Gently stir until smooth. Chill for 1-2 hours.

Use a small ice cream scoop or melon baller to scoop out truffles. You can roll them in your palms for a few seconds to smooth out the shape, but work quick as the heat from your hands will melt them.

Roll the truffles in toasted coconut and place on a tray lined with waxed paper or parchment paper. Return to the fridge for 30 minutes to firm up again. Store in an airtight container in the fridge for up to 2 weeks.

*using raw coconut oil will add some more coconut flavor to the truffles

Makes 10-15 truffles, depending on size

Dark Chocolate Coffee Truffles

4 oz. dark chocolate, chopped

4 T. heavy cream

¼ tsp. vanilla extract

1 tsp. unsalted butter

1 T. chopped coffee beans

Place coffee beans and cream in a jar with a lid. Let steep in the fridge for 20-24 hours, swirling occasionally (it will be thick). Strain the beans from the cream and set aside.

Place chopped chocolate in a heat proof bowl. Heat the cream and butter in a small saucepan until just to a simmer. Pour warm cream mixture over chocolate and let sit for 1-2 minutes. Add vanilla extract and stir gently until smooth. Refrigerate for 30-60 minutes.

Scoop out truffles with a small ice cream scoop or melon baller. You can roll them in your palms to create a smoother shape, but work quickly as the heat from your hands will melt the chocolate.

Roll the truffles in your choice of toppings (or leave them bare): Cocoa powder, toasted coconut, or toasted chopped hazelnuts

Variation: Substitute 1 T. of the cream for Irish cream, Kahlua, hazelnut liqueur, almond liqueur, or Irish whiskey

Makes 10-15 truffles, depending on size

Cold Brew Crepes

½ c. cold brew concentrate

½ c. milk

2 eggs

1/8 tsp. salt

1 c. flour

2 T. melted butter

2 tsp. cocoa powder

Place all ingredients in a blender and whirl until combined. Chill in the refrigerator at least 30 minutes.

Heat a non-stick skillet over medium heat. Place ¼ c. of batter in the pan and swirl it gently so the bottom of the pan is thinly coated (about 3-4 mm thick). When the edges begin to look dry and some bubbles appear on the top surface, carefully flip the crepe over and cook for another 30-60 seconds. Often your first crepe is ugly but edible. Consider it practice, and a tasty bonus for the chef.

Serve rolled up with a dollop of Kahlua spiked whipped cream and fruit (optional)

To make Kahlua spiked cream: Whip 1 c. heavy cream with an electric mixer until soft peaks form. Add 2 T. Kahlua and run the mixer for a few more seconds to combine. Alternately, if you are using canned whipped cream, squirt a few tablespoons worth into a bowl, add a splash of Kahlua and stir it in.

Makes about 6 crepes

Cold Brew Crème Brulee

1 c. heavy cream

½ c. coffee beans

2 egg yolks

2 T. sugar

½ tsp. vanilla extract

Sugar or brown sugar

Place the coffee and cream in a jar with a lid. Let steep in the refrigerator for 20-24 hours, swirling occasionally. Strain out the coffee.

Preheat the oven to 300 F. Heat the cream to barely a simmer in a saucepan. In a separate heatproof bowl whisk together egg yolks and sugar. Slowly add cream, whisking continuously. It is important to start adding the cream to the eggs very slowly to avoid scrambling the eggs. Return the entire mixture to the saucepan and stir 2-3 minutes until slightly thickened.

Divide the cream into ramekins and bake 25-35 minutes in a water bath. If your ramekins are shallow, bake for about 25 minutes, if you have deeper ramekins, you may need to leave them in the oven for up to 35 minutes. They should be set and not jiggle much when done. Remove from the oven and chill thoroughly.

To serve, remove chilled crème brulees from the fridge and place on a baking sheet. Sprinkle a thin coating of sugar or brown sugar over each crème brulee (about 2 tsp. each). If you have a kitchen torch, briefly torch the sugar until lightly brown and caramelized.

If you do not have a kitchen torch, place the baking sheet with the crème brulees under the oven broiler until the sugar starts to bubble and turn caramel colored. This will warm the crème brulee more than the torch method. You may want to return the crème brulees to the fridge for 15-30 minutes to re-chill before serving.

Makes 2 creme brulees (about 4 oz ramekins)

Mocha Frosting for Brownies

2 c. icing sugar (confectioners sugar)

¼ c. butter, room temperature

2 T. cold brew concentrate

1 T. cocoa powder

½ tsp. vanilla extract

Place all ingredients in a bowl and mix with an electric mixer until smooth and fluffy. Make your favorite brownie recipe from scratch or from a box and let cool. Top with this creamy frosting and see how long they last.

Variation: Use the coffee butter below as your butter in this recipe

Coffee Butter

2 c. heavy cream (at least 35% milkfat)

1 c. coffee beans, roughly chopped

Stand mixer or strong arms

Place coffee and cream in a jar with a lid. Let steep in the fridge for 20-24 hours, swirling occasionally. Strain out the coffee.

Place the cream in the bowl of a stand mixer fitted with a whisk attachment. Start whipping the cream, after 4-5 minutes you should have whipped cream. Continue whipping until the cream gets stiff and the butter starts to separate from the buttermilk and stick to the whisk. Discard the buttermilk (or use it for something else).

Place the butter in a cheesecloth lined strainer. Pick up the ends of the cheesecloth and squeeze any excess buttermilk from the butter until you can't get any more liquid out of it.

References

1. All About Coffee, William Ukers https://www.gutenberg.org/files/28500/28500-h/28500-h.htm

2. https://coldbrewqueen.com/japanese-pour-over-ice-method-iced-coffee-in-a-hurry/

3. https://coldbrewqueen.com/nitro-cold-brew-coffee/

4. https://scienceandfooducla.wordpress.com/2014/08/19/coffee-brewing-chemistry-hot-brew-and-cold-brew/

5. Modernist Cuisine vol. 4, Maxine Bilet and Nathan Myrhvold

6. http://www.scanews.coffee/2014/07/11/coffee-roasting-chemistry-chlorogenic-acids/

7. http://www.healthline.com/nutrition/top-13-evidence-based-health-benefits-of-coffee#section13

About the author

Renae Clark is an author and serial entrepreneur. Although she has always considered herself a dilettante (since discovering the word), she doesn't just dabble, she takes a deep dive into whatever she is obsessing over at the time. When she read the 4 Hour Work Week, she was not so much struck by the idea of only having to work 4 hours, but with the 36 extra hours a week she could use to pursue her hobbies and passions. This is her first book about one of those passions, which combined her more recent love of cold brew with her years of baking and cooking experience in developing the recipes. She also writes online business books on topics related to her entrepreneurial journey.

A favor: Small indie authors sometimes have a hard time having their books be found (especially those of us who cringe at self-promotion).

Reviews help other customers know whether this book is right for them, and also helps books get found in search results. If you have the time to share your thoughts by leaving a review of this book, it would be very much appreciated.

Recipe Index

Mocha Syrup	49
Peppermint Cocoa Creamer	28
Peppermint Cold Brew Cloud	33
Rhode Island Coffee Milk	24
Spiced Syrup	25
Spiked Cream	32
Toasted Coconut Cold Brew Coffee	20
Vanilla Creamer	26
Vanilla Sweet Cream Cold Brew	29
Vietnamese Iced Milk Coffee	39
White Chocolate Coconut Truffles	50

Made in the USA
Las Vegas, NV
30 November 2020